D1222289

The Library of
NATIVE AMERICANS

The Ojibwe

of Michigan, Wisconsin, Minnesota, and North Dakota

Janet Palazzo-Craig

The Rosen Publishing Group's
PowerKids Press™
New York

Special thanks to Kevin L. Callahan
for his help and guidance in the making of this book

Published in 2005 by The Rosen Publishing Group, Inc.
29 East 21st Street, New York, NY 10010

Photo and Illustration Credits: Cover © HIP/Scala/Art Resource, NY; p. 4 Mindy Liu; p. 6 © Raymond Gehman/Corbis; p. 9 William Armstrong/NATIONAL ARCHIVES OF CANADA/C-010645; p. 10 Musée de l'Histoire Naturelle/Bridgeman Art Library; p. 12 Library of Congress, Geography and Map Division; p. 15 © Bettmann/Corbis; p. 16 © The New York Public Library/Art Resource, NY; p. 19 General Research Division, New York Public Library Astor, Lenox, and Tilden Foundations; pp. 21, 27, 31, 36 Minnesota Historical Society; p. 22 © Lowell Georgia/Corbis; p. 25 © Corbis; p. 32 © Réunion des Musées Nationaux/Art Resource, NY; p. 35 Hulton Archive/Getty Images; p. 38 © Werner Forman/Art Resource, NY; p. 40 Picture Collection, The Branch Libraries, The New York Public Library, Astor, Lenox and Tilden Foundations; p. 42 © Smithsonian American Art Museum, Washington, DC/Art Resource, NY; p. 45 © North Wind Picture Archives; p. 47 The Detroit Institute of the Arts, USA/Bridgeman Art Library; p. 48 Catalogue No. 366453, Department of Anthropology, Smithsonian Institution; p. 50 © Ed Kashi/Corbis; p. 53 Time Life Pictures/Getty Images; p. 54 © Joseph Sohm/Corbis.

Book Design: Erica Clendening
Book Layout, Ojibwe Art, and Production: Mindy Liu
Contributing Editor: Kevin Somers

Library of Congress Cataloging-in-Publication Data

Palazzo-Craig, Janet.
    The Ojibwe of Michigan, Wisconsin, Minnesota, and North Dakota / by Janet Palazzo-Craig.
    p. cm. — (The library of Native Americans)
    Includes bibliographical references and index.
    ISBN 1-4042-2873-X (lib. bdg.)
    1.Ojibwa Indians—History—Juvenile literature. 2.Ojibwa Indians—First contact with Europeans—Juvenile literature. 3. Ojibwa Indians—Social life and customs—Juvenile literature. I. Title. II. Series.

    E99.C6P35 2005
    977.004'97333—dc22
                                                                    2003028133

Manufactured in the United States of America

There are a variety of terminologies that have been employed when writing about Native Americans. There are sometimes differences between the original language used by a Native American group for certain names or vocabulary and the anglicized or modernized versions of such names or terms. Although this book contains terms that we feel will be most recognizable to our readership, there may also exist synonymous or native words that are preferred by certain speakers.

Contents

Where the Ojibwe Live

North Dakota

Minnesota

Wisconsin

Michigan

Canada

United States

Atlantic Ocean

Gulf of Mexico

One

An Introduction to the Ojibwe

Let's journey to the Great Lakes region of the United States. Look out across the wide, cold waters of these five vast lakes. Walk among the tall trees of the forests. Then try to imagine a time long ago when a way of life, far different than ours, existed for the people of these forests. These inhabitants were the Ojibwe, one of the groups of Native Americans who dominated the region.

The Ojibwe culture is based on the belief that nature is full of gifts that have been given by the spirits. For a very long time, the Ojibwe's ability to function in nature, taking only what they needed in order to survive, guaranteed that there would always be enough resources. Tools, food, shelter, and clothing were provided by nature. The Ojibwe greatly respected these gifts.

How did these people, who treasured the earth so much, come to be known as the Ojibwe? No one knows for sure, but there are many theories. One theory is that the word Ojibwe means "puckered up." This may refer to the unique sewing style that once was used for making Ojibwe moccasins. The seam of the moccasins was gathered up in the front and had a puckered look. Later moccasins made by the tribe did not have this seam, however. Other spellings of the group's name are Ojibway and Ojibwa. Yet another

This map shows the Ojibwe homelands surrounding the Great Lakes within the United States.

Among other means of expressing ideas, the Ojibwe created pictographs. A pictograph, such as this one from northern Minnesota, is a painting on a rock. This Ojibwe pictograph shows a human figure standing with a moose and another animal, possibly a dog or a wolf.

is Otchipwe. When Europeans heard the name, they mispronounced it as Chippewa. That name was used on many treaties and other documents between the tribe and the United States government. Thus, Chippewa became another common name for these Native Americans. In more recent times, the name Ojibwe or Anishinaabe, meaning "first people" or "original people," has been preferred by many tribal members as the authentic name.

Another theory about the origin of the tribe's name is that it comes from a word that means "people who make pictographs." Pictographs are drawings that usually represent words or specific ideas. Sometimes they represent dreams and visions. The Ojibwe are known for creating such drawings. Their medicine men and women drew pictographs on birch bark as a way to keep records and remember songs and ceremonies.

How did these "first people" come to live in the vast woodlands near the lakes? The Ojibwe settled near the Great Lakes more than 500 years ago on land that now makes up the states of Michigan, Wisconsin, and Minnesota, as well as parts of southern Canada around the lakes. Farther west, the Ojibwe came to occupy parts of what is now the state of North Dakota. Although many of today's Ojibwe still live in these places, their way of life has greatly changed. These changes began when the tribe started to trade with Europeans, the first being the French. Today there are still many Ojibwe who seek to preserve the old customs and beliefs of their unique tribe.

In the past, the seasons of the year greatly affected the life of the Ojibwe people because of the changing weather conditions. The tribe learned they needed to move from place to place in order to survive. Depending upon the season, the people knew where to gather food, hunt, fish, or plant gardens. During these seasonal migrations, the Ojibwe traveled to the marshes, streams, and forests of the Great Lakes. They traveled on foot and by canoe, depending upon their destination and the type of resources they were seeking. This aspect of tribal life developed over many years. Let's learn more about the early history of the Ojibwe and how it shaped their culture and life ways.

In 1901, William Armstrong painted this watercolor scene of travelers on the Great Lakes. In the painting we can see a European-style boat with an Ojibwe canoe.

Two

Early History

The Ojibwe came to be an important and dominant tribe in the Great Lakes region in the 1500s. Why did the Ojibwe settle in this region? What do we know about the earliest history of this group?

Many scholars believe that before arriving near the Great Lakes, the ancestors of the Ojibwe and of other Native Americans traveled over a bridge of land. This migration took place 13,000 to 40,000 years ago, although the exact dates are unknown. The strip of land traveled by these people connected Asia and Alaska. After crossing from Asia to North America, these people moved to the east and to the south, becoming the continent's first inhabitants. These ancient natives of North America were hunters. They followed caribou, giant mammoths, oxen, and other large prey as they moved across the land.

Many people believe that the Ojibwe originally lived in the east, near the Atlantic Ocean and the mouth of the St. Lawrence River. Others think that the tribe first lived in the north of Canada by Hudson Bay. Not much is known about this period, but it is thought that these early people used sleds pulled by dogs to travel in winter. They moved overland to hunt and to gather food. They may also have had canoes and may have planted corn.

Herds of animals such as the woolly mammoth once roamed North America. The early people who lived here relied on these and other animals for food.

According to Ojibwe oral history and tradition, when the Ojibwe were living on the East Coast near the Atlantic Ocean the prophet of the First Fire told the people that they must move or they would be destroyed. Oral history is the passing down of stories by word of mouth from generation to generation. In response to this prophecy, a great migration took place over several hundred years. The migration, which began about 900 A.D., would eventually lead the Ojibwe across the Great Lakes.

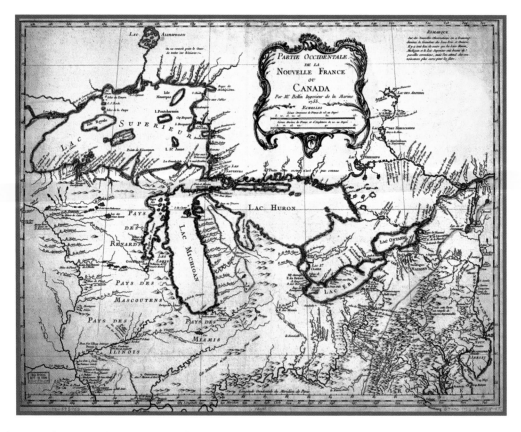

12 This is a hand-colored map of the Great Lakes region published in 1755. It was created for France by Jacques Nicolas Bellin.

When they reached the place where Lakes Superior, Huron, and Michigan almost touch, these Native Americans split into three groups. These are the Ojibwe, the Potawatomi, and the Ottawa tribes. These Anishinaabe tribes are known as the Nation of the Three Fires, or the Three Fires Confederacy. The Ojibwe are the Keepers of the Faith. The Potawatomi are the Keepers of the Sacred Fire. The Ottawa are the Trader People.

During the migrations, the Ojibwe encountered several enemies. These were the tribes of the Six Nations of the Iroquois Confederacy. The Three Fires Confederacy tribes fought battles with the Asakiwaki, or Sauks, and the Mesquakie, or Foxes, during the migration. In the Midwest, battles with the Dakota tribe took place.

After reaching the Great Lakes region, most of the Ojibwe followed the lifestyle of the forests. Those that moved to North Dakota, however, took up the culture and way of life of the Plains Indians. The Ojibwe became the largest tribe of Native Americans occupying this huge region of North America.

The language that a group of people speaks is very important in defining their culture. The Ojibwe language has several related subgroups of languages. All of them originally come from the Algonquian group of languages. The Algonquian languages are a family of more than 30 languages. They are spoken by many different tribes in northern North America. Many Ojibwe words have become part of the English language. For example, the words moccasin, Mississippi, and moose come from the Ojibwe language.

The Ojibwe's activities were linked very closely to the seasons of the year. This was because each season presented its own challenges for survival. The Ojibwe found ways to adapt to each season, using what nature provided at each time of year to give them food and shelter. The forests were full of animals most of the year, and bountiful hunting gave the Native Americans ample meat to eat and skins for clothing. Spring provided plentiful fish and maple sugar, made from the sap of maple trees. Summer brought many kinds of berries and ripening corn. In fall, the Ojibwe gathered wild rice, an important part of their diet. In winter, they hunted deer or rabbit. They also ate the rice they had stored.

Later, when the Ojibwe came into contact with Europeans, their culture started to change. They began to trade with the newcomers. The Ojibwe often traded furs for blankets and metal tools. Life changed as the native people substituted these ready-made objects for items they had formerly made themselves. Hunting for furs to trade also changed the tribe's relationship with the natural world. Instead of hunting for only what they needed, the Ojibwe began to hunt additional animals in order to trade the skins with the Europeans.

The Ojibwe became the largest group of Native American traders. The people lived in bands composed of several families. There were separate leaders for each band, and the bands moved from place to place for much of the year. They returned to more permanent dwellings during the rest of the year. The Ojibwe had, and still have, a system of clans within their bands. Each person is born into the extended family of the clan and is not allowed to marry within the clan. The people trace their family ancestry through the father's side. In early times, the members of the band had a strong sense of community. They knew they needed to work together to survive the harsh winters of the northern country. The bountiful forests, however, helped to ensure their survival. In the pages that follow, we'll discover more about their survival methods.

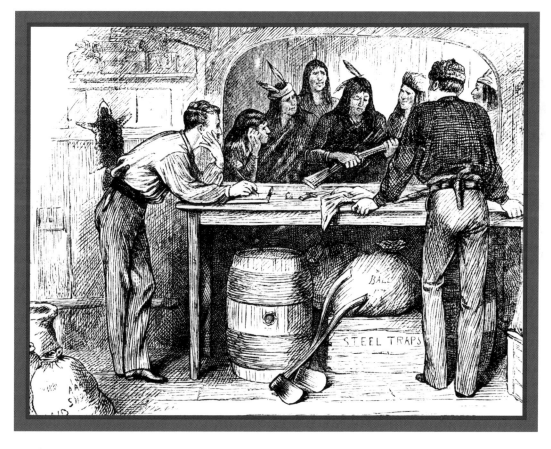

This nineteenth-century woodcut shows how a British trading post in the Great Lakes region might have looked. The goods traded at these posts would completely change the Ojibwe way of life.

Three

Life Among the Ojibwe

The Ojibwe were a resourceful people who made the most of what the forests, lakes, rivers, and marshes of the Great Lakes region had to offer. Firmly rooted in this people's culture was a deep respect for nature. They believed that the land, water, plants, and animals were gifts. The land could not belong to anyone. It was there for all to use in a respectful manner that was not wasteful.

A change in the weather as a new season approached meant a change in lifestyle for the Ojibwe. The tribe marked time by observing the phases of the moon. They named the months after the moon and the kind of weather or natural event that was known to occur during that time. For example, Deep Snow Moon was the name of the month we call February. May was called the Moon of Flowers, and September was called the Moon of Falling Leaves.

In early spring, the snow and ice began to melt. It was March, the Moon of Snowblindness. The people knew it was time to pack their clothes and tools and move to the maple forests, also called the sugar bush. It was time for the maple sap to run through the trees. The Ojibwe would tap into the trees and collect the sap, from which they would make a year's supply of maple sugar and syrup.

This artwork shows an Ojibwe man spearfishing through the ice. In his left hand, he holds a stick that has a wooden fish lure at one end. In his right hand, he has his spear ready to strike the fish.

While moving to the sugar bush to set up camp, the bands used the backs of their dogs or toboggans to transport their belongings. When they reached the maple trees, they moved into longhouses that they built in seasons past. A longhouse was a dwelling that stood in a clearing. The longhouse had a wooden frame that was covered with birch-bark strips. Several families would occupy the longhouse during sugaring. It was a happy time, for the bands had not seen each other during the long, cold winter. They enjoyed reuniting and socializing.

To collect the sweet sap, an Ojibwe woman took a cedar chip and drove it into the tree trunk. Then she cut a gash into the trunk above the cedar chip. A birch-bark container was placed below the gash. As the sap flowed inside the tree, it flowed out of the gash and was collected in the container. The small containers of sap were emptied into larger ones. Then the sap was heated and cooked by putting very hot rocks into the liquid. Later, iron kettles were used, and a fire was set beneath them to heat the sap. The boiling sap became thick syrup. Some of this was used, but most of the syrup continued to cook and became maple sugar. This sugar could be stored and used throughout the year. It was used as candy and as a seasoning for fish, wild rice, and vegetables.

When the weather became warmer, it signaled the beginning of summer. The Ojibwe prepared to leave their longhouses. They would return to these dwellings next spring. The tribe now journeyed to the many lakes and rivers of the region. Setting up camp, the

This Seth Eastman illustration of a sugar camp was originally published in *The American Aboriginal Portfolio* in 1853. The dwelling that Eastman pictures here is a wigwam. The wigwam is one of several kinds of dwellings the Ojibwe used.

people planted gardens. Corn, squash, potatoes, and beans were grown. The women also gathered food, such as raspberries, strawberries, and blueberries. It was also time for them to find and pick herbs and plants that could be used as medicines. Fish were extremely plentiful at this time of year, and the men of the tribe spent most of the season fishing. The Ojibwe fished from their canoes by spearing the fish, or by using nets. Some of their catch was smoked or dried and stored away.

When the weather began to turn cooler, fall began. The Ojibwe bands traveled once again, this time to the marshes where wild rice could be harvested. Each clan returned to the same area each fall. Wild rice was an extremely important part of the Ojibwe diet because it could be easily stored and used throughout the year.

To harvest the wild rice, the people used canoes. Two people worked together. One paddled the canoe while the other used a stick to bend the stalks of the plants. A second stick was used to hit the plants. This loosened the rice kernels, and they fell into the canoe. Afterward the rice was spread upon birch bark and dried. Then the husks were removed. The Ojibwe did this either by stamping on the husks or hitting them with long sticks. The rice was then tossed into the air to separate the grains of rice from the husks. The husks were light and blew away during this process. The grains were heavier and fell together in a pile. The natives used bags made of birch bark to store the rice.

In the mid-1880s, Alfred Zimmerman photographed these Ojibwe women while they were out on their canoe gathering wild rice. This method of gathering wild rice is still used today in northern Minnesota.

Before long, the weather turned colder. Signs of the approaching winter, which was usually very snowy and cold, told the Ojibwe it was time to move to their winter camps in the forests. They moved back into domed wigwams. A wigwam was built with one or two holes in its roof to let out the smoke from the fires used to keep warm and to cook.

Work baskets, such as this one, were made and used by Ojibwe women who worked during the winter to make clothes and household items. This basket holds strips of leather and a pair of child-size moccasins.

The women used the winter months to make clothes. They used animal hides for this purpose. Household items, such as mats, bags, and baskets, were also crafted. Many of these items were made from birch bark.

The Ojibwe did their hunting in the winter because they knew that in the spring and summer many baby animals are born. The Ojibwe hunters did not want to take the mothers from their babies because then the supply of animals would decrease. The Ojibwe hunted ducks and other waterfowl, or birds. They also hunted deer, bear, moose, and wolves. They used traps or snares to catch smaller animals, such as fox, beaver, mink, otter, muskrat, and rabbit. The Ojibwe also used bows and arrows to hunt. After they began trading with the Europeans, steel traps and guns were also used.

The winter months were a time to share stories about the tribe's past. The elders entertained the youngsters with amusing and wise tales as the family sat around the fire on cold nights. These winter evening activities helped the young members of the Ojibwe band learn about their past and about the beliefs of their people.

The Ojibwe of North Dakota lived in a different style than other Ojibwe bands. The Bungee of North Dakota and other Ojibwe bands of the West, extending into what is today the state of Montana, adopted the ways of other Plains natives. This is called the buffalo culture because the people's lives centered on the buffalo as their main resource. These Ojibwe depended upon the buffalo for food, shelter, dress, and other items. Their art and ceremonies were also different from the Ojibwe of the Great Lakes region. The people lived a nomadic life, always on the move as they followed the buffalo migration. They hunted buffalo with great skill, never killing more than what they needed. The tipis in which the natives lived were easily taken down and transported, which suited their way of life very well.

Traditional Everyday Life

What was everyday life like in the past centuries for the Ojibwe? What kinds of homes did they build? What did they eat? How did they dress? All of these daily activities were important aspects of Ojibwe life.

The bands of Ojibwe, moving from place to place with the changing seasons, had a variety of dwellings. The most permanent of their homes was the dome-shaped wigwam. This remarkable dwelling was quick to build and kept families cool and dry in the summer and warm in the winter. A wigwam measured about 12 feet in diameter. It was oval shaped or round and was built upon a frame of long poles, which were bent to form the dome of the building. It was the women's job to lash the poles together. They used twine they made from the tough inner fibers of bark, and they also used strong strips of leather. To cover the frame, the Ojibwes overlapped cattail mats they had woven or sheets of birch bark. A hole or two in the center of the ceiling was used to vent smoke from the fire. A leather skin was placed over another opening that served as a door. This flap worked well to keep out the wind.

Inside the wigwams, mats were placed on the floors and hung on the walls to protect the inhabitants from the cold. The mats were woven from stemmed marsh plants called bulrush. Bedding consisted of blankets, deer hides, pillows filled with duck feathers, and bearskins. During the day, the people rolled up their bedding and used it as a cushion to sit against.

Ojibwe make the dome-shaped wigwams in this illustration from 1884. Note the framework of bent poles that the woman to the right is lashing together.

Other types of wigwams used by the Ojibwe were longhouses similar to the kind made by the Iroquois people, who lived to the east. The longhouses were bark-covered lodges like the wigwams, but were longer and could fit more people. Yet other dwellings were tipis, similar to the kind built by the tribes to the west, such as the Cheyenne and the Dakota. These dwellings were cone shaped and were covered with animal skins. Tipis were temporary homes and could be taken down and easily transported from place to place during a hunting trip.

The diet of the Ojibwe was a varied one, as much of what they ate depended on the season of the year. They hunted moose, deer, bear, rabbit, and ducks with which to make stews. The stews were seasoned with wild ginger, dried berries, mountain mint, and pumpkin blossoms that had been dried. Fish was also eaten, either fresh or dried and smoked. Fish could also be frozen and stored when it was caught during the winter.

Wild rice was the tribe's most important grain, but the women also grew corn. They used a rounded stone to grind the corn into a coarse meal that was used in a lot of recipes, including one for bread. The maple sugar that was made in the spring was used to make a cool summer drink and also to season foods, since the natives did not have salt. The women also grew squash, beans, and potatoes in their gardens.

The Ojibwe especially liked wild berries, such as raspberries, cranberrries, and strawberries. They also collected wild herbs, which they used to season food and to prepare medicines.

It was the women's job to make clothes for all the members of the tribe. They tanned the hides of deer to make leather to sew into garments. They also used the skins of rabbit, squirrel, and beaver. Decorations were very important to the Ojibwe. They were skilled at making beautiful designs on their clothes. At first, they used porcupine quills, shells, and feathers to make these designs. After they began to trade, they acquired beads that they sewed into colorful patterns and pictures.

Fur robes, made from the skins of bear and deer,

Wizard

This young Ojibwe woman is dressed for the winter. The patchwork on her coat is a good example of the type of beautifully designed patterns worked into Ojibwe clothing.

were worn by both women and men during the cold months. The natives also lined their moccasins with cattail down or fur to make them warmer.

Sinew was used as thread to sew the seams of leather garments. The tough sinew was strong. The women used a sharp bone to punch holes in the leather through which they sewed the sinew. Women wore buckskin leggings and leather dresses. The men wore breech-cloths, shirts, and leggings. Children's clothes were very tight because the Ojibwe believed this would help the youngsters grow with a straight, strong back.

Both men and women wore their hair long and used bear grease to make it shine. The men wore eagle feathers in their hair as a sign of their courage. Women wore their hair wound tightly against their scalps or wove it into two braided pieces. The braids were some-times decorated with otter fur.

Cultural Roles and Activities

The roles that women and men played as adults in the Ojibwe tribe were roles that were taught to them from childhood. When a baby was born, it was cherished. A medicine man or woman might be asked to give the baby a name based on a dream or vision. The baby might be given a name that had to do with a special event, a unique characteristic, or an animal. Because boys would grow up to be hunters, their names sometimes had to do with this activity. A child would also be given a common name or nickname. This name was usually a short name such as Little Twig or Grasshopper. However, sometimes children would simply be named after someone else. Many times a dream name would be given to a boy during a vision he might have as part of a ceremony where he was required to fast, or to go without food. Although this name would seldom be spoken, it had great spiritual meaning.

Girls were taught to stay near the tribe's camp where they learned how to build wigwams and to cook. They also helped their mothers sew clothes and make baskets. They took part in the various harvests, as well.

Boys learned the habits of animals and of the woodlands. Courage and independent behavior were taught. The tribe celebrated when a boy successfully hunted his first big animal.

After corn and other crops were planted, both boys and girls had the job of scaring away the birds and animals that might try to eat the crops.

For men and women, their adult roles followed the lessons of their youth. Women built wigwams, sewed clothes, grew gardens, and harvested wild rice and other plants. Men were the hunters and warriors. The Ojibwe did not often fight with other tribes. One of the main reasons for this was because great distances separated the Ojibwe from others. Disputes did occur at times, though. As warriors, the Ojibwe would quietly stalk and quickly attack their enemies, often by surprise.

Canoes were an important way of traveling for the Ojibwe, and their light, strong canoes were extremely well made. A wife and husband worked together to create a canoe.

The family was the center of village life, and the time when the most bands lived together was during the summer months. Each family traced its heritage from groups called clans. The clans were usually named after animals and birds.

During the winter months, families entertained themselves by sitting around the fire inside the wigwams and telling stories. These stories were often funny or exciting and they also served to teach the children about the tribe's values and history. Courage and respect for nature were taught, as well as the importance of listening to one's elders in order to learn. Winter was a time for games as well. In bad weather, the children played inside with stone marbles and dolls made from cornhusks. They also had tops and toy canoes.

During a snowfall, the children often had snowball fights. They played a game called snow-snake, in which they slid sticks across the crusty ice and snow. The object of the game was to see how far one could slide the stick.

Life for Ojibwe families, such as the people in this 1910 photograph, centered around the wigwam. These lodges gave the family shelter as well as a place for playing games and telling stories, especially during the winter months.

Four

Contact with Europeans

The Ojibwe had already been living in the region of the Great Lakes for more than 100 years before their first contact with European explorers. It is believed that one of the first meetings between the two took place in the early 1600s. At that time, the Ojibwe may have met the French explorer Samuel de Champlain. Other French explorers in the area called the Ojibwe Saulteurs, a word that means "people who live near the rapids." This is because the French encountered the tribe near the rapids at Bowating, in present-day Michigan. The city at the rapids is called Sault Sainte Marie today.

Other contact with the French occurred when fur traders and missionaries came to the region in ever larger numbers in the 1640s. Ojibwe who did not like the Europeans moved away to the west. Other Ojibwe found that the French traders were peaceful people. Some French men married Ojibwe women and embraced the Ojibwe way of life. Nevertheless, the beginning of trade between the two cultures meant that Ojibwe life would begin to change. As the Ojibwe came to rely on the ready-made blankets, metal tools, and weapons they got from the Europeans, they began to overtrap the forests in search of pelts to trade. To overtrap is to

Artist Theodore Gudin shows a group of early French explorers and a group of Ojibwe greeting one another in this painting from 1847.

kill too many animals, causing the animal population to decrease. This went against the Ojibwe belief of living in balance with nature, and it would greatly affect the tribe's future.

The Ojibwe made a trade agreement with the French in 1679. Frenchman Daniel Greysolon, Sieur du Lhut, helped to make the agreement. The city of Duluth, Minnesota, is named for him. The trade agreement created Grand Portage Trading Post in what is now northeastern Minnesota. The Ojibwe agreed to trap furs and then trade them at the trading post and also to serve as middlemen between the French and traders of the Dakota tribe. To expand their hunting territory and to control more rice marshes, the Ojibwe successfully waged war with several tribes of Native Americans, including the Dakota and the Mesquakie (Fox).

Unlike many other native tribes, the Ojibwe had very few bloody wars with the European settlers who came to the New World. The Ojibwe did, however, side with the French during the French and Indian Wars, which were waged against the British from 1689 to 1763. Unfortunately for the Ojibwe, the French lost the dispute and the tribe was left to deal with the British, who did not like them for siding with the French. The British outlawed trade with the Ojibwe, and the tribe experienced many hardships, because they had come to rely on traded goods. This led the Ojibwe to join other tribes in an unsuccessful uprising against the British in 1763. As part of an effort for a peaceful future, the British agreed to allow native peoples to stay in their homelands. This was important for the Ojibwe, for they occupied a huge area in the Great Lakes region by the late 1700s.

As more and more American settlers pushed into Ojibwe territory, the natives allied themselves with the British to help keep away newcomers. After the British lost to the Americans in the American Revolutionary War, the Ojibwe had to give up much of their land.

By 1815, millions of acres of land had been taken from the Ojibwe by the U.S. government in a series of treaties. A small portion of the land was used to create reservations upon which the Ojibwe would live. At that time, the Ojibwe also suffered enormous loss of life due to disease. They did not

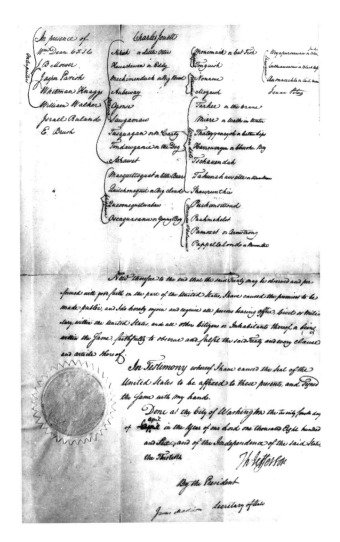

This 1806 treaty between the United States government and the Ojibwe was signed by President Thomas Jefferson. The treaty has a U.S. government seal on it.

These Ojibwe women and children from a Minnesota reservation were photographed in 1904. The picture was taken in the Minnesota Forest Reserve. This was later re-named Chippewa National Forest.

have immunity to many diseases carried by the settlers, such as smallpox and measles.

The Ojibwe, unlike most other native groups, were not removed far west of the Mississippi River by the U.S. government. The Ojibwe reservations were small, but they were still located within the tribe's original region. The Ojibwe also kept their rights to hunt and fish. In 1867, the reservation known as White Earth was created for the Ojibwe. It is the largest reservation in Minnesota. Wisconsin and Canada are also home to Ojibwe reservations. In the United States, the government expected the Ojibwe to become farmers. However, the land on these reservations, while being ideal for hunting and fishing, was not proper for farming. Furthermore, the Ojibwe lacked the skills needed to farm and in many cases chose not to become farmers. Yet without the wide territory they once roamed, the tribe could no longer hunt and trap or follow other seasonal activities. Hunger, illness, and hardship became a way of life. Some Ojibwe decided to leave the reservations. They moved to large cities, taking jobs and living in Western culture. This further decreased the Ojibwe population on the reservation.

For a time, native children were forced to leave their families and go to schools where they were expected to learn English and to adopt Western clothes and customs. At last, after World War II, the U.S. government, acting through the Bureau of Indian Affairs, began to grant more freedom of choice to the Ojibwe. Fortunately, some of the native people had kept the knowledge and culture of the tribe alive, so not all of this valuable heritage and way of life was lost.

Five

Religion and Art

The Ojibwe traditionally believed that the Great Spirit, called Kitche Manitou, created the world. According to Ojibwe belief, many other spirits also exist in nature. The Ojibwe honored and gave thanks to the spirits by offering them food and pinches of tobacco. For the Ojibwe, religion was a deeply personal experience.

A special society existed among the Ojibwe. It was dedicated to honoring and keeping alive the knowledge given by the spirits, especially that given by Kitche Manitou. This special group is the Grand Medicine Society, also called the Midéwiwin.

Both women and men became part of this society. First, they spent many days learning about the special healing powers of herbs and charms. This was followed by many initiation ceremonies. It was the job of the Midéwiwin to heal people both physically and spiritually. The members of the society drew upon their powerful connections to the spirits. In dreams or visions, they called for guidance in choosing the proper herb or charm from their medicine bags in order to help the ailing.

Rituals and ceremonies also existed for other members of the tribe. When a baby was born, the clan members were very happy. They made a lot of noise as they rejoiced, because they believed

This Ojibwe wood figurine is from Leech Lake, Minnesota. The carving is believed to have been used by an Ojibwe healer.

40 Charles Bird King painted this Ojibwe mother holding her child's cradle board. Note the hoop above the child's head. This was to hold a blanket or cloth to keep the child's head protected throughout various weather conditions.

that the child would be very brave if she or he was used to loud noises. Traditionally, the baby was securely bound to a cradle board for a year. The family believed that the board would help the child's back grow strong and straight. Several times a day, the mother took the baby out of the cradle board for exercise and cleaning. Charms were hung from the cradle board above the baby's head to protect the child from harmful spirits.

When a boy came of age and was about to become a man, his father took him on a vision quest. The boy was told to fast. Then the boy was left for several days in a shelter in the woods. His father would come to check on him periodically. The purpose of the vision quest was for the young man to have a special dream. The dream would reveal to him what he would do in life and which guardian spirit or spirits would be his. As part of becoming a man, the boy would also hunt an animal for the family to feast upon. This was a much-celebrated event.

When two young people wished to marry, the young man hunted a large animal to give as a gift to the young woman's family. If he was invited to feast with them, this meant the marriage could take place. There was no formal ceremony. At first, the couple lived with the woman's family for a year or more. Then the couple set up their own housekeeping. If after a year, the couple wished to divorce, the woman returned to her former life with her family.

The traditions and rituals surrounding the death of a family member varied between the different Ojibwe bands. In one known tradition, when someone died the family officially grieved for a year. The Ojibwe wrapped the body in a blanket and birch bark and they might have painted the dead person's face either red or brown. The Ojibwe then had a spiritual leader lead a ceremony. The people believed the deceased would then travel for four days.

42 George Catlin shows what an Ojibwe ceremonial dance may have looked like in this oil painting from the late 1830s.

Food was placed with the body to help it on its journey. The clan members buried the body with the feet facing west. It was believed that the direction of the setting sun was where the spirits lived. The Ojibwe believed in an afterlife where there is a land of beauty with abundant game and sparkling waters. Upon reaching this afterlife, the deceased is reunited with other dead clan members.

Many dances were also a part of the rituals and ceremonies of the Ojibwe. A war dance was held before a battle, and a victory dance took place afterward. Ceremonies, songs, and dances also existed to give thanks for the rice harvest. Medicine men sang special songs to protect hunters or to ensure a good harvest. A sweat lodge was also a part of the band's community. This special structure was used for purification and healing rituals.

Legends and Myths of the Ojibwe

The Ojibwe told legends about the many spirits they believed in. Many of these tales explain things that occur in nature. Others tell how the Ojibwe first learned about the bounty of the natural world. One hero is found in many such legends. His name is Winabozo, also known as Waynaboozho or Winabojo. He is often described as both a trickster and a hero. The stories tell how he discovered many of nature's gifts that he gave to the Ojibwe.

Winabozo Discovers Wild Rice

One day, when Winabozo was a boy, his grandmother came to him. "Grandson," she said, "the time has come for you to go into the forest. Do not eat; fast for a time. It will give you extra power."

Winabozo set off for the forest, carrying his bow and arrows. After many days, he came to a beautiful lake. All around the lake grew a lovely, graceful, yet simple-looking plant. The boy had never seen this sort of plant before.

"How beautiful!" exclaimed Winabozo. "I will bring Grandmother here to see this plant."

The boy returned with his grandmother, and the two collected seeds from the plant. They did not know it, but the pretty plants were wild rice. Then the old woman and her grandson went to another lake, where they planted the seeds. Winabozo returned to the forest and continued to fast. When he grew light headed from lack of food, he heard a plant say, "At times, we are food for others."

Winabozo ate the plant, but he soon became very sick from it, and he could not move. When at last he was strong enough to go on, another plant said, "At times, we are food for others." This time, though, Winabozo did not eat the plant for fear of becoming ill.

Upon reaching a river, another plant spoke to the very hungry boy, offering itself as food. By this time, Winabozo was extremely hungry. "I must eat," he said. He shook the grains from the plant and tried them. They were delicious, and this time he did not feel ill. Happy at his discovery of the tasty plant, Winabozo looked closely at it. To his surprise, it was the same sort of plant that he and his grandmother had planted—it was the wild rice plant!

Winabozo hurried back to his grandmother and the rice plants they had planted. He told her of his discovery, and from that day on the Ojibwe have eaten the gift of wild rice.

This birch-bark basket holds the traditional wild rice the Ojibwe harvest to this day.

Stories such as that of Winabozo are still told today in order to teach young Ojibwe the customs and beliefs of their tribe. The legends also tell of the Great Spirit, Kitche Manitou, who created the world. It is said that the creation was done in four stages. Kitche Manitou first made the rocks, wind, fire, and water. Next, he created the sun, earth, stars, and moon. Then came the first plants. At last, animals and people were created.

Other spirits of the Ojibwe included the powers of the directions of north, east, south, and west. Additional spirits were believed to exist in animals, rocks, trees, and other parts of nature. Good spirits, found in lightning and thunder, were said to bring wisdom. Evil spirits, including witches and ghosts, also existed and were said to bring harm.

Arts and Crafts

The Ojibwe culture was rich with many arts and crafts that are both useful and beautifully made. Baskets, jewelry, clothing, as well as pictographs, canoes, and tools, were just a few such works of art. Special songs and dances have also been created by the Ojibwe for ceremonial uses.

The birch-bark canoes made by the Ojibwe were light, beautiful, and very strong. The knowledge of how to make such canoes has been kept alive through the years. As in the past, some Ojibwe canoes still are made by hand. The frame of the canoe is made of

The richness of the Ojibwe crafts can be seen in works such as this shoulder bag from the 1850s. The bag was made from wool, yarn, silk, cotton thread, and glass beads.

48 This is a dental pictograph made by an Ojibwe woman. Dental pictographs were made by biting soft, folded birch bark.

white cedar. It is covered with sheets of birch bark and then sewn together with spruce tree roots. The seams are sealed with pine gum to make them watertight.

Birch bark has traditionally been used for many other purposes by the Ojibwe. Trays, containers for rice that are decorated with beautiful cutout designs, and buckets used to collect maple sap are three examples.

Clothing, such as leggings, aprons, or moccasins, and other objects were decorated with feathers, dyed porcupine quills, shells, and beads. Designs inspired by nature, such as flower or leaf patterns, were typical. Beaded leather and feather headdresses and bags, bracelets, and necklaces are a few of the lovely pieces that were worn for ceremonial dances and songs. The men's dance outfits often had red tassels made of horsehair. Body painting among the men for religious ceremonies was another art form. Men's jewelry for such occasions might have included nose rings and brass armbands.

One very special art form of the Ojibwe was called a dental pictograph. By folding a piece of birch bark and biting into it, beautiful designs were revealed when the bark was unfolded. The Ojibwe healers also drew pictographs. These pictures served various functions. They helped healers remember the way certain songs must be sung. In this way, the pictographs functioned as a form of writing.

Six

The Ojibwe Today

Today, many Ojibwe are dedicated to keeping alive their unique culture and beliefs. Ojibwe who have left the reservations, as well as those who live modern lives on the reservations, are working to pass on traditional values, skills, and culture to the younger generations.

At gatherings known as powwows, Ojibwe clan members, other Native Americans, and non-native visitors are invited to meet. Ojibwe arts and crafts are shown. Traditional stories are told and dances, songs, and ceremonies take place. Young Ojibwe girls and boys dressed in traditional clothes often take active roles at the powwows. Drum and dance groups compete. Traditional foods are served. These meetings help to share the culture with others and also to keep alive its importance among the Ojibwe.

In addition to their rich cultural legacy, the Ojibwe have produced clan members who have made important contributions. For example, Dakota and Ojibwe activists established the American Indian Movement (AIM) in 1968. This group worked to make the public aware of treaty violations that the U.S. government committed. The movement was also dedicated to making the Ojibwe and other native groups proud of their art and heritage.

Ojibwe youngsters enjoy themselves at a full dress powwow on the Lac Courte Oreilles Chippewa Reservation, Wisconsin.

The Ojibwe have also produced fine writers, such as Louise Erdrich, Gerald Vizenor, John Tebbel, Jane Johnston Schoolcraft, and William Whipple Warren. Warren's studies of Ojibwe history are one important source of information about the past culture and history of the group.

Today, the Ojibwe number about 50,000 in the United States. There are reservations in Michigan, North Dakota, Wisconsin, and Minnesota. The largest is called White Earth, located in Minnesota. In the United States, the Ojibwe are the third biggest native tribe. Approximately 150,000 Ojibwe live in Canada.

Through the years, more than half of all the Ojibwe have left the reservations. Many of those who left went on to successful jobs and careers in cities such as Minneapolis, Chicago, and Milwaukee. Some returned to the reservations to retire after successful careers. Others who left went to college or trade schools and became teachers, nurses, and skilled workers. They returned to the reservations, bringing their skills with them to help other tribe members improve their standard of living. Some began small industries and campgrounds for tourists on the reservations. Craftspeople, wilderness guides, camp counselors, and fishermen also earn their living on the reservations. Another portion of the Ojibwe population still gathers wild rice and produces maple sugar. They survive by living on the land, much as their ancestors did. Other Ojibwe work on the committees and in the tribal government agencies that run the reservations.

The Ojibwe have faced many problems over the years. Poverty, illness, and unemployment have been major obstacles for native people living on the reservations. With time, though, the Ojibwe have gained more and more control over their lives on the reservations and have been able to improve many difficult conditions. Natives have also set up casinos, which have greatly helped the Ojibwe economy by providing jobs and money. The tribe has made very wise investments with the profits from the casinos by buying back lands that were formerly part of Ojibwe territory. The casinos also support health centers, schools, and government agencies. Ojibwe colleges have also been founded.

Louise Erdrich is famous for her works of poetry and fiction, which include her best-selling novels *The Beet Queen*, *Tracks*, and *The Bingo Palace*.

The Ojibwe are proud of their cultural legacy. The Ojibwe language, arts, history, and ceremonies are valuable treasures. Clan members are determined to work together to keep this

knowledge alive and to share with other cultures their great respect for the natural world.

A number of regions around the Great Lakes, such as this Minnesota shoreline of Lake Superior, are still home to many Ojibwe people.

Timeline

13,000 to 40,000 years ago	Ancestors of the Ojibwe journey to North America from Asia.
900–1500	The Ojibwe arrive and settle in the Great Lakes region.
Early 1600s	Ojibwe first encounter Europeans, probably French traders.
1679	Grand Portage Trading Post is established. The Ojibwe become middlemen between Dakota native groups and French traders.
1689–1763	The Ojibwe ally themselves with the French against the British in the conflicts leading up to and during the French and Indian Wars, which end in defeat of the French. The British refuse to trade with the Ojibwe for a time after the war, causing the tribe great hardship.

1776	The Ojibwe become allies of the British during the American Revolutionary War.
1815–1855	The Ojibwe negotiate to stay on their lands in Michigan, Wisconsin, and Minnesota, while ceding much territory to settlers. Many more treaties follow, in which the Ojibwe are forced to cede more land.
1867	To make more land available to non-natives, White Earth Reservation is created.
1968	The American Indian Movement (AIM) is established in Minneapolis, Minnesota. Many Ojibwe begin to take part in the Native American civil rights movement. Their major goals are to secure rights for natives and to recover lands taken away by treaties.
1988	Gambling becomes legal on the reservations, and the Ojibwe build casinos on their U.S. reservations. The casinos provide jobs and revenue for the Ojibwe.

Glossary

activist (AK-tiv-ist) A person who acts to bring about change for a cause.

afterlife (AF-tur-life) Life after death.

breechcloth (BREECH-cloth) Long, narrow pieces of animal skins pulled up between a man's legs and fastened with a narrow belt around the waist.

casino (KUH-see-noh) A building or room used for gambling.

cattails (KAT-taylz) Tall, thin plants with long, brown, furry pods at the top and narrow leaves.

confederacy (kuhn-FEH-duh-ruh-see) A group of people or nations that are united and share the same beliefs.

cradle board (KRAY-duhl bord) A board about two feet long, with a curved piece of wood at one end and a hoop at the other, used to hold infants and help them grow straight.

customs (KUHSS-tuhms) The traditions in a culture.

heritage (HER-uh-tij) Valuable or important traditions handed down from generation to generation.

immunity (i-MYOON-uh-tee) Protection against a disease.

inhabitants (in-HAB-uh-tants) The people who live in a place.

legacy (LEG-uh-see) Something handed down from one generation to the next.

migration (MYE-gray-shuhn) The act of moving from one region to another.

nomadic (NOH-mad-ik) Wandering from place to place.

pelts (PELTZ) Animal skins with the fur still on them.

pictograph (PIK-toh-graf) A painted or drawn picture used as a symbol.

prophecy (PROF-uh-see) A prediction.

rapids (RAP-idz) A place in a river where the water flows fast.

reservation (rez-ur-VAY-shuhn) An area of land set aside by the government for a special purpose, as in a tribal reservation.

reunite (ree-YOO-nite) To bring together again.

ritual (RICH-oo-uhl) A set of actions that is always performed in the same way as part of a religious ceremony or social custom.

sinew (SIN-yoo) A strong fiber or band of tissue that connects a muscle to a bone; a tendon.

snow blindness (SNOH BLINDE-ness) Unable to see due to light reflecting off the snow.

tipis (TEE-peez) Dwellings that have frameworks of poles covered by bark or cloth.

Resources

BOOKS

Benton-Banai, Edward. *The Mishomis Book: The Voice of the Ojibway*. Hayward, WI: Indian Country Communications, Inc., 1988.

Bial, Raymond. *The Ojibwe*. Tarrytown, NY: Benchmark Books, 1999.

Bleeker, Sonia. *The Chippewa Indians: Rice Gatherers of the Great Lakes*. New York: Wm. Morrow and Co., 1955.

Broker, Ignatia. *Night Flying Woman: An Ojibway Narrative*. St. Paul, MN: Minnesota Historical Society Press, 1983.

Child, Brenda J., *Boarding School Seasons: American Indian Families, 1900–1940*. Lincoln, NE: University of Nebraska Press, 2000.

Danziger, Edmund Jefferson, Jr. *The Chippewas of Lake Superior*. Norman, OK: University of Oklahoma Press, 1990.

Densmore, Frances. *Chippewa Customs*. St. Paul, MN: Minnesota Historical Society Press, 1979.

Greene, Jacqueline Dembar. *The Chippewa.* New York: Scholastic Library Publishing, 1993.

Hilger, M. Inez. *Chippewa Child Life and Its Cultural Background.* St. Paul, MN: Minnesota Historical Society Press, 1992.

Kohl, Johann George. *Kitchi-Gami: Life Among the Lake Superior Ojibway.* St. Paul, MN: Minnesota Historical Society Press, 1985.

Osinski, Alice. *The Chippewa.* New York: Scholastic Library Publishing, 1987.

Stan, Susan. *The Ojibwe.* Vero Beach, FL: Rourke Publishing, LLC, 1990.

Warren, William W. *History of the Ojibway People.* St. Paul, MN: Minnesota Historical Society Press, 1984.

Wheeler, M. J. *First Came the Indians.* New York: Atheneum, 1983.

Wolfson, Evelyn. *From Abenaki to Zuni: A Dictionary of Native American Tribes.* New York: Walker & Co., 1988.

ORGANIZATIONS

Bad River Tribal Council
P.O. Box 39
Odanah, WI 54861
(715) 682-6679

Mille Lacs Band of Ojibwe Indians
HCR 67, Box 194
Onamia, MN 56359
(612) 532-4181

WEB SITES

Due to the changing nature of Internet links, PowerKids Press has developed an online list of Web sites related to the subject of this book. This site is updated regularly. Please use this link to access the site:

http://www.powerkidslinks.com/lna/ojibwe

Index